To Tom Davis, VMI '64

[signature]

House Mountain Affair by Harry Hathaway Warner

© 2015 by Harry Hathaway Warner. All rights reserved.

No part of this book may be reproduced in any written, electronic, recording, or photocopying form without written permission of the author, Harry Hathaway Warner.

ISBN: 978-0-9830752-2-6
Library of Congress Control Number: 2015946484

Published by Alone Mill Media, Lexington, VA

Printed in USA

House Mountain Affair

A Personal Journal and Pictorial Study of the Signature Landmark of Lexington, Virginia
By
Harry Hathaway Warner

Front Cover Painting by Cabell Warner Gorman

Note by Author: I chose this unusual impressionistic and whimsical rendering of House Mountain by my daughter because its luminous colors perfectly correlate with the female connotations of
my imaginary affair with House Mountain.

The back cover is a photograph (circa late 1940's) of a train entering Lexington by backing up over the Maury River. House Mountain is prominent in the background. The railroad was completed in 1881, but there was no way for trains to turn around as the tracks dead-ended at the station in the town. They had to be reversed at a section of track shaped like an inverted "Y" about a half-mile from the bridge and then backed up across the river through W & L and VMI. In those days, the students took great pleasure in greasing the tracks, making it difficult for a train to back up the steep grade behind the schools. The trestle bridge was destroyed and the line abandon in 1969 after Hurricane Camille.

This book is published in association with
The Rockbridge Area Conservation Council.

RACC's non-profit mission is to promote the wise stewardship and sustainable use of natural and cultural resources in the Rockbridge area, including to preserve the natural habitat and perpetuate the traditional uses of House Mountain; that is, hiking, hunting, bird watching and the like.

All proceeds from its sale and any associated contributions will go toward fulfilling its mission primarily as it relates to House Mountain.

Dedication

To my wife, Sis, for sticking with me through the blessings and challenges of fifty-five years of marriage, fostering four children and seven grandchildren, while all along putting up with my idiosyncrasies including my
HOUSE MOUNTAIN AFFAIR.

ACKNOWLEDGEMENTS

Having had the concept for this book for decades, I have had encouragement when mentioning it from too many people to remember them here by name. I apologize for this necessary omission, but salute them without attribution.

The writing and construction of the book has been greatly enhanced by the skills of two people:
Rob Walker of Richmond has, for the second time in my publishing efforts, brought his considerable editing skills, experience and wisdom to bear on the writing and production process. Probably, his greatest challenge again has been to convince me that more is not better and conciseness counts.

My meeting of Amanda Loreti was serendipitous. She is a native of Rockbridge County and a House Mountain aficionado. She has put in endless hours in computer design, layout and photographs. As these are not my basic skills, I could not have produced the book without her assistance.

Laurie Lipscomb was critical in the final photo enhancement, production and publishing. Anne McClung, as an accomplished author, provided excellent guidance.

I would also like to thank Ed Spencer and Bruce Summers, both members of the RACC board, who reviewed early drafts and gave encouragement.

Typical Scenery about Lexington from *Lexington in Old Virginia*
Henry Boley, 1936

Table of Contents

I	Introduction	1
II	Community Portrait	17
III	Transfiguration by Circumnavigation	41
IV	Spiritual Connotations	51
V	Fanciful Facsimiles	57
VI	Sunrises	61
VII	Sunsets	65
VIII	Clouds	71
IX	Moons	75
X	Four Seasons	79
XI	Notable Scenes and Items	85
XII	Epilogue	99
XIII	References	105

Section I
Introduction

AN AFFAIR OF A LIFETIME

This book represents a personal quest or journey if you will. Hence the word "journal" is used in the title to describe it. I have had an "affair" with House Mountain, Lexington's (and Rockbridge County's) monolithic natural sculpture, stretching over sixty years, and in the latter half of that time frame I have dreamed of paying homage to it. The affair began like so many boy-girl love affairs in that I was not initially impressed with the object of my later affection. That most certainly was due to my circumstances at that time.

RAT

In September 1953, I matriculated from Staunton, Virginia, to the Virginia Military Institute to enter as a 4th classman or freshman into its notorious "Rat Line." For those uninformed about this training phenomenon, it was in those days like opening and entering the Gates of Hell. Other than its renowned honor system, the Rat system was the most defining characteristic of one's experience at the Institute. The honor code was and still is based on two basic rules: "A cadet will not lie, cheat or steal nor tolerate those who do." Dismissal was the only penalty for a violation and was carried out at that time in a dramatic and brutal "drumming-out" ceremony in front of the entire corps in the middle of the night. The first time a Rat witnessed the ceremony it would be etched forever on his mind.

The Rat year lasted from matriculation to around May 15, during which there was constant organized and personal harassment and intimidation from upper classmen. While in the cadet barracks Rats had to walk the Rat Line in an exaggerated shoulders-back-and-chin-in position and had to run up all stairs. Events were organized to instill a little extra discipline. For instance, "the Big Circle," was when at night you ran up four flights of stairs in the barracks, across the top (fourth) stoop, down the steps, below the barracks, through a room full of steam from running showers, back to the starting point. Then do it all over about 10 times. The kicker was that it was done while wearing thick rubberized rain

Section 1: Introduction

capes, which made the running more difficult and exacerbated the sweat. Another example was "Bloody Sunday" held a week before getting out of the Rat Line. That was a day when any upperclassmen could tell you to bend over and give as many whacks as he deemed appropriate with a paddle, bent coat hanger or some other device.

However, it was the personal attention that a Rat received that really wore him down. Woe to a Rat to get on the wrong side of an upper classman who might take him on as his personal target for misery. The whole idea was to tear you down and then give you the opportunity to rebuild yourself and more in the three remaining years of your cadetship. It was an endurance and survival test of the first order that stayed with you for the rest of your life. For example, one alumnus, who was a World War II European Theatre veteran, was quoted in a newspaper article that having lived through his Rat year, he knew he could get through the Battle of the Bulge. That may have been a little hyperbolic, but it demonstrates the mind set of VMI alumni after experiencing the Rat Line.

The old model of adversative training at VMI, including the Rat Line and honor dismissals, is not practiced as severely today because of our modern litigious society and the court-ordered enrollment of females at the Institute in 1997. The Rat Line is now much shorter in duration and more of a positive military training experience with less personal harassment and no events like the Big Circle or Bloody Sunday. In terms of today's standards it is still a challenge, and the cadets know House Mountain better than we did because part of their organized kinder and gentler Rat training is the requirement to team climb the Mountain at its steepest slope as visible from Lexington. On my many hikes up there it has taken two to three hours, depending on what grandchild is with me and what stage of my aging capabilities I am in. I have seen present day Rats do it in forty minutes.

As it has been for 175 years, when the Corps marches out on the parade ground for drill or even more so for a formal dress parade there House Mountain is present to its far right, adding to the pomp and circumstance of the review. I think the VMI cadets may be more aware of House Mountain than the students at contiguous Washington and Lee University who don't have a good campus view of it and don't go through a Rat Line that requires climbing it.

Section 1: Introduction

My Rat experience set the stage for the beginning of House Mountain becoming a life-long object of my attention. When the two battalions of the Corps formed up there was a series of bugle calls over a period of four minutes or so leading up to the formations – "first call," "big toot," "little toot," "shake-a-leg" and "assembly", blown by two professional buglers named Bill and Tony. Upper classmen would rarely appear before the first notes of assembly, and frequently the buglers would drag out its playing to allow a few stragglers to avoid demerits for being late to ranks. Rats were required to be in ranks by big toot, and the only upper classmen to arrive that early were the 3rd class corporals who used the advance time to inspect and verbally abuse the Rats.

That was something to be endured by Rats at every Corps formation, and I learned to focus on things out on the horizon while keeping my head straight. A basic Rat safety rule was to achieve anonymity by not drawing attention to yourself and moving your head in ranks was a prime attention getter. In those days there were no buildings at the far end of the parade ground to gaze at, but I found I could cut my eyes to the right to focus on mighty House Mountain. Thus began my affair with the mountain, which I used as a mental escape device.

THE AFFAIR IS ENHANCED

I maintained an association with VMI after graduation, but my memory of House Mountain waned. It was not until twenty-one years later, after a career in commercial banking in Richmond and as president of Transohio Financial Corporation in Ohio, that it was rekindled. I returned to Lexington in 1978 to become the executive vice president of the VMI Foundation and to manage the Institute's first endowment fund raising campaign. I was delighted to return to Virginia and, being a Valley boy, to be back home. My office was located in a house on Letcher Avenue just outside the VMI Post's limits gates and we leased a house at 450 Institute Hill at the opposite end of the Post. Every morning as I drove past the parade ground to work I would view House Mountain, and that reignited my old affinity. It was then that I first observed that the Mountain seemed never to look the same on any given morning.

During this time I began a family ritual that extends to this day. It became a coming-of-age requirement for my children and later my grandchildren to climb the face of House Mountain with me and spend the night. It began in 1980 when my

Section 1: Introduction

two daughters, Cabell and Ann, and I hiked up and camped on the small space on Little House overlook. (See note below.) They were ages 17 and 15 respectively, and it was a great way to spend time with them at that age. Part of our family lore is the story of Cabell diligently mixing hamburger meat with onions and other veggies and wrapping them in tin foil to be cooked for dinner by throwing them in a fire, but she forgot to put them in her pack. Ann was the savior of the evening meal as she had just in case, packed a can of Dinty Moore Stew, one of my favorites for camping outdoors. When I gave the picture of the two girls shown on page 16 to them, I wrote on the back, "You can climb any mountain!" I meant that metaphorically and they both, in fact, have climbed some pretty challenging ones in their adult lives.

By this time my oldest son, Harry Jr., had left home for college, the Army and his career so he has not climbed House with me. I have climbed and spent the night on House with my other son, Patrick and grandchildren Patrick Gorman (before his untimely and tragic death in 2010), Jack Gorman, Olivia Warner and Mary Elizabeth Warner. The only exceptions for the granddaughters were that I had my daughter, Ann, accompany us. We hiked down to the Saddle between Big and Little House Mountains where there is a shelter to spend the night as opposed to camping on the cramped outcropping of the Little House Overlook. It was fortuitous that Ann was with me as I found that my usual pack had an age-related-miraculous increase in weight and I had to switch with her for her lighter pack.

For the grandchildren who make the climb I have developed an "Award of Accomplishment" certificate, which I present to them at family reunions. I recently made my final-grandchild-climb with Fox Warner, age 12, Hank Warner, age 11 and Ryland Warner, age 10, up the face to the Little House Overlook. We then traversed the top of Little House to the Saddle, camped out, and came back down the regular trail where we had left a car. My 18-year-old grandson, Jack, who will be a Rat at VMI this Fall, served as my "first sergeant" for the climb as he had contractually agreed to do when I gave him my 1999 Chevrolet Silverado pick-up truck. I have a sense of satisfaction of having completed the climb with all the grandchildren, especially since, at facing 80 in a few months, I am running out of steam.

Note: The "Little House overlook" is my identification of the distinctive rock outcrop and cliff on the north east end of Little House Mountain. The legendary "Student Rock" is varyingly claimed by locals to be located either at the high point in the center of Little House or approximately one third of the way down the mountain from that point..

Section 1: Introduction

PENIEL FARM

In 1981, another serendipitous event happened that had great ramifications for my life and in its own way cemented my relationship with the mountain. It is a story worth telling. I had been given an American Pointer hunting dog, and I was most excited because, although I grew up hunting quail, I had never owned a hunting dog. Bea was a sweetheart, had a great nose for birds and knew just how to cover a field.

My predecessor and mentor at the VMI Foundation was Joe Neikirk who lived in a lovely white house, now owned by Washington and Lee University, at the intersection of Nelson Street (Route 60 West) and West Denny Circle. Right across Nelson Street was an undeveloped and overgrown parcel of approximately eight acres. Joe introduced me to this as an excellent location for an upscale real estate development. I, indeed, later acquired the property on which to develop a townhouse project to be known as Sixty West.

One Sunday in 1981, I decided to walk Bea over this rough property to give her some exercise, maybe flush some birds and to inspect it more closely. To my surprise she walked across Route 60 and went west fifty yards to another piece of property. I followed her and noticed that it had a nice pond by the road. At the top of the hill I was blown away by the 360 degree view of the Blue Ridge to the East and the familiar Jump and Hog Back mountains to the West. More importantly, there was the best view of House Mountain that I had ever seen. Instantly, I was in love with the property. I followed Bea over a second hill and discovered a bold spring, a nice creek and about a quarter of a mile of frontage on the Maury River including a deep swimming hole with a natural sandy beach. I also realized that, although I felt that I was way out in the country, I was only about four driving minutes from Main Street in Lexington. I decided right then that I had to have this property.

The land was owned by two elderly sisters, a Ms. Seebert and a Ms. Boyden. The land had been in their family since 1911. Joe Neikirk introduced me to them and we began a long waltz as I negotiated the purchase of the property. In 1984, I obtained a three-year option to buy it. I worked on and enjoyed it as if I owned it, but for financial reasons let the option expire. Later I kicked myself for that and went back to them to try to buy the property outright. When I went up to the ladies

Section 1: Introduction

rocking on the front porch of their nineteenth century Jacktown Road farm house, Ms. Seebert, who was about 88 and only about five feet tall, said, "You don't mean at the same price do you?". When we closed on the purchase in 1989 my wife, Sis, proclaimed that those little old ladies were a lot smarter than I was.

When I stepped down from the VMI Foundation the next year to pursue a lifelong dream of being in business for myself, the new farm helped keep the flame of my House Mountain affair alive. Although for development and marketing purposes we lived in one of the Sixty West townhouses, I spent innumerable hours working on the farm property. We had previously owned three farms – two in Ohio and one in the Estaline Valley near Goshen – so I was familiar with the challenges and vagaries of operating a farm with cattle and horses. However, I had never taken on a piece of property so run down and overgrown with Osage orange trees (in my opinion the worst tree God made) and cedars, and with no fencing, barn or house. As I began to improve the property I put a gazebo on top of the hill to have cookouts and adult beverages, but more importantly to gaze out on changing weather, storms in the distance, the spectacular night skies, lightening, rainbows, the Blue Ridge Mountains, and Lexington's northwestern mountain sisters – Jump, Hogback, Big Butt and especially House.

I named the property "Peniel Farm," which is admittedly strange. I came up with that in 1983 long before acquiring it. This is from a journal I wrote about properties I have owned: "I was sitting on the porch of our house on Institute Hill reading the King James Bible. I came across Genesis 32:30 – 'And Jacob called the place Peniel: for I have seen God face to face, and my life is preserved.' I immediately made a vow that if I ever owned the Seebert property and developed it into a gentleman's farm I would name it Peniel Farm. My reasoning was that, by owning the land (land Biblically is given great importance) and looking out from it to the wonderful vistas, I could see God face to face and that would help preserve my life." Later, I found that the language of that passage in other versions of the Bible indicate that Jacob's life was preserved in spite of his seeing God's face, not because of it. That interpretation didn't deter me from my commitment to the farm's name and in 1998 I erected a sign at the entrance, which remains there today even though I no longer own the property.

Section 1: Introduction

THE AFFAIR IN BLOOM

It wasn't until 1999 that we began construction of a house on the farm. I served as the contractor and used the same subcontractors we had at the Sixty West development. My previous improvements over the years included clearing, tearing down an old house, erecting board fencing, putting in a hard surface driveway to the house site and constructing a twelve-stall stable, equipment barn, riding ring and parking lot. We did everything backwards as our house was the last thing to be built, but we were committed to living in Sixty West until it was fully developed. One of my requirements for the new house was that it have a tower for my home office that had 360 degree views. Indeed, my desk looked directly toward a marvelous view of House Mountain. Another requirement was that I be able to see House from where I sat to watch TV in the den. We accomplished that also with the view through a large picture window. We completed work on the farmhouse about the time I closed my office in Lexington and kind of retired. I was then 65 and decided if we got ten years of living on the farm, I would be happy. We actually got almost eleven, and like Jacob, I think our lives were preserved by the constant awareness of landscapes and sky.

The state of my romance with House Mountain changed during the decade we lived on Peniel Farm from 2000 to 2011. It ripened and fully bloomed. Particularly in the first several years after we moved into our dream house, I couldn't get over our constant perspective of it. I observed as I had living on Institute Hill that its look changed constantly. Of course, it wasn't changing itself except seasonally, but the weather, the clouds, the sun, the moon, the rain and the snow created different and often spectacular shows endlessly. Being in such an advantageous place I could look out the window any time and see what was up at the Mountain. That allowed me frequently to run get my camera and take a shot of it. I developed a portfolio of amateur pictures of the Mountain and other great natural scenes from our amazing vantage point. I, indeed, achieved a "House Mountain high".

In a classic-old-age downsize I sold the entire property to Washington and Lee in December 2010 and rented the house back for six months. Although never expecting it, but now pleasantly living back at our development, Sixty West, I miss the farm every day, though I don't at my age miss the responsibilities of upkeep, maintenance, managing help, etc.

Section 1: Introduction

AN AFFAIR TO REMEMBER

I am now in the stage of fostering fond memories of my affair. Producing this book is a way to capture them permanently and at the same time puff them up to enhance them. Living out of sight of the Mountain makes it more difficult to sense if there is a photo opportunity. To achieve that these days requires a round trip walk of one to three miles or a drive of some distance, and in the end possibly being disappointed. But all romances contain some pain, particularly in their waning days.

I am a closet writer. Since my retirement fifteen years ago, I have written much material for my own portfolio on subjects from my career, people whom I have known and philosophical/theological interests. In 2013 I published a book, "A Young Life of Light," about my grandson and oldest grandchild who died tragically at almost 18 years old on my 75th birthday, November 30, 2010. He was an unusual young man who overcame serious disabilities as a child to become an accomplished fisherman, shooter and artist. More importantly, in spite of his disabilities, he made a huge impact on his peers, a fact which did not come fully to light until his death. His life was a gift and publishing my story about him was an added gift from him.

After completing this book on House Mountain, I may have one more in me that I have been writing off and on for years. It is a comprehensive consolidation of my thoughts on the imponderables of life. If I make it to age 80 with faculties intact I may complete it. Whereas the book on my late grandson was a labor of love and this book is a labor of amusement, the third is a labor of life. I read once that people work so hard to leave a tangible estate to their children, but leave little of themselves. Well, my children and grandchildren may be disappointed in the amount of their financial inheritances but are going to be overwhelmed by the written material I am leaving them. If they do read it, it will confirm that the old man was more than a little daffy, and that's okay. As with all writers I am myself the matter of my book (Michel de Montaigne), and I can't worry about what my legacy will be.

To my amazement none of the local libraries - Rockbridge Regional, W&L or VMI - has anything of note about House Mountain in its collections. In all three, when using their computer-driven-research-index files there are no titles or

Section 1: Introduction

key words when "House Mountain" is entered. W&L has several accounts by student climbers from the 19th century and several newspaper articles, but that's it! Obviously, the Mountain, much to my surprise, may not have had the impact on others that it has had on me. That makes this book unique, a fact that pleases and unnerves me at the same time.

It may be peculiar to have an on and off lifelong affair with a mountain, but given that human affairs can get one into a heap of trouble this is an attraction from which I have taken much pleasure and no risk. Indeed, Sis not only has been aware of my affair she has encouraged it. If my personal journal is not creditable, informative or amusing I hope you enjoy the written and pictorial presentation on the Mountain itself, which I trust demonstrates my underlying themes – its character, majesty and visual variability. Although it is perpetual in a structural sense, its appearance is anything but constant as it is ever changing from the effects of the seasons, the weather and its interface with the sun and the night skies.

The photographs by others are chosen for their excellence. My own pictures, even if honest, are somewhat amateurish. They were taken to demonstrate the Mountain's nature and not as artistic renderings of which I am incapable. My only saving grace is the optical power of the subject. With these caveats, I hope that you will find "House Mountain Affair" entertaining and edifying.

For blocks are better cleft with wedges,
Than tools of sharp or subtle edges,
And dullest nonsense has been found,
By some to be the most profound.

Samuel Butler, poet (1612-1680)

Section 1: Introduction

House Mountain Overlooking VMI
Photo by Michele Fletcher

Section 1: Introduction

Peniel Farm with House Mountain in the Background

Section 1: Introduction

Peniel Farm's Ancient Osage Orange Tree Clings to Life Under the Watchful Eye of House Mountain

Section 1: Introduction

Home on the Range Where the Deer and the Horses Play. Taken from Peniel Farm Tower Office

Section 1: Introduction

Peniel Farm was no Monticello, but the variable observational experiences of nature were like those eloquently described by Thomas Jefferson in 1786:

How sublime to look down into the workhouse of nature, to see her clouds, hail, snow, rain, thunder all fabricated at our feet! And the glorious Sun when rising as if out of a distant water, just gilding the tops of the mountains and giving full lie to all nature.

Section 1: Introduction

Every mountain top is within reach if you just keep climbing.
Barry Finlay, *Kilimanjaro and Beyond*

It is not the mountain we conquer but ourselves.
Edmund Hillary, *mountaineer and explorer*

Daughters, Cabell and Ann, 1980

Granddaughters, Mary Elizabeth and Olivia, 2012

Conquering House Mountain

Section 1: Introduction

View from Rock Overlook at North East End of Little House

Section II
Community Portrait

ROCKBRIDGE COUNTY

The beauty of the Valley of Virginia is uncontested. Any time Sis and I return to Lexington from Dulles Airport from a trip to some place in the world we comment that we didn't see any scenery more beautiful than that we were passing through on Interstate 81. The highway, a main artery, already carries excessive traffic and there is unfortunate talk of widening it. However, it does give a superb view of the Valley from Winchester to Roanoke. Traveling south one observes that the Valley perceptively narrows from its expanse of rolling countryside in Augusta County to a closer relationship with the bordering mountains in Rockbridge. There is a sense that the Blue Ridge and the Alleghenies are more intimate in Lexington than they are in Staunton. Rockbridge County, in addition to being located in this heavenly part of the world, is blessed with many natural features including mountain streams and pristine rivers, the most prominent of which is the Maury River.

UNIQUE GEOLOGICAL FEATURES

Beyond its general natural attractiveness, Rockbridge County contains several unique geological features in addition to House Mountain. The Natural Bridge is its most famous. A 215-foot limestone arch known to the Monacan Indians as the "Bridge of God", was surveyed by George Washington in 1750 (the initials "GW" seen 23 feet above the level of the creek under the bridge were purportedly carved by him) and owned by Thomas Jefferson from 1774 until his death in 1826. In Notes on the State of Virginia, Jefferson described Natural Bridge as "the most sublime of nature's works." It is a National Historic Landmark, Virginia Historical Landmark, is listed in the national Register of Historic Places and is a major tourist attraction.

In February 2014, a significant transaction took place that should preserve Natural Bridge and its surrounding land in its natural state in perpetuity. After being owned privately for centuries, the bridge and a contiguous 188 acres are now owned by a non-profit organization, the Virginia Conservation Legacy Fund. It is the intention of the Fund ultimately to transfer this real estate plus an additional 1,300 surrounding acres to the Commonwealth of Virginia all to be owned and operated as a state park. The commercial properties supporting visiting tourists will continue to be owned and operated privately.

Another unique natural phenomenon in the county is Devils Marbleyard – a mountain of truck-size chunks of boulders looking as if a giant had knocked over a display of massive building blocks. Originally sands formed on a beach that existed in this area a half a billion years ago, they were later compacted into a quartzite layer. About 200 million years ago the quartzite layer cracked as a collision took place between North America and Africa. More recently the cracked quartzite began to slip down the slope creating the massive pile of rocks. Although the site is visited by intrepid hikers, either jumping from rock to rock or creeping upward on all fours balancing from one sharp boulder to the next, it is not for the faint-hearted, children or the infirm.

Goshen Pass is also famous as a natural and beautiful gorge between Goshen and Rockbridge Baths where the Maury River roars through it over large rocks. Oren F. Morton in his book, *A History of Rockbridge County*, wrote an apt description of it in 1920:

> *The river is constantly flowing over or among masses of rock and is in a continuous cascade. A new vista opens with every bend in the road, and the stranger who goes from one end of the pass to the other and then retraces his steps finds the return nearly as replete with interest as the advance. There is not a house and not an acre of tilled land within in the pass, and the view is well-nigh as primeval as it was in the day of the Indian.*

LEXINGTON

Lexington, the Rockbridge County seat, is both compatible with and contrary to the county. With the exception of Lexington and the more industrial city, Buena Vista, the county is primarily rural and farm oriented supplemented by tourism and small businesses. The city of Lexington is small, quaint, diverse, slow to change, and culturally polished.

Section II: Community Portrait

In a flowery description of 19th century flavor, in his 1935 book, Henry Boley in his book, *Lexington in Old Virginia*, after enumerating every Southern city of note, says:

> *…but none excel in sentimental interest as this little Athens of the Old South….*

> *Seen from Reservoir Hill on a summer afternoon, nestling among trees like a jewel in a perfect setting of green fields and wooded country, with the everlasting hills forming a great amphitheater, Lexington suggests Elysium. A Visitor of long ago claimed that the scenery was unsurpassed and lovely beyond description…. Visitors have compared the countryside to rural England, to southern France, to Switzerland and to other God-favored places.*

He also declares:

> *One Sunday afternoon last spring while sitting all alone in the sunroom listening to the immortal Ninth Symphony of Beethoven as the sun was setting in all its majesty behind Brushy Hills, the thought came to me; fortunate is he whose lot is so pleasantly cast: music, magnificent scenery, fine fellowships, abiding friendships and, in fact, everything that makes life worth living. All of these and more one has in Lexington.*

One can make all but the same claim about life in Lexington today. Yes, it is literally and figuratively wired into the 21st century, but most of Mr. Boley's pleasant conditions still exist.

Lexington's economy and social structure are considerably influenced by its two colleges, Virginia Military Institute and Washington and Lee University, which are located contiguous to each other but which could not be more different. The other leg of its three-legged economic stool is tourism. As influenced by the college faculties, the town is politically liberal when compared to the conservative county residents. It is steeped in Confederate Civil War history with its two most famous citizens being Robert E. Lee and Thomas J. "Stonewall" Jackson. Unlike the county, Lexington in recent years has downplayed this heritage as deemed a "politically incorrect" liability. Under Virginia law the city is governed separately from the county, which can be both a blessing (independence) and a curse (financial challenges). The Virginia Horse Center located in the county close to Lexington is a significant public relations and financial resource for both.

The one area in which the city and county are in complete unison is in appreciation of the natural beauty of the area and its amazing valley/mountain landscapes. The support for environmental organizations such as the Rockbridge Area Conservation Council and the Valley Conservation Council is strong in the city and the county. City and county residents, particularly those who live in its shadow, equally appreciate House Mountain.

One other little recognized factor about Lexington is that it is the intersection of two old significant roads: U.S. Route 60 that runs all the way from Virginia Beach to California and U.S. Route 11 that runs from Montreal, Canada to New Orleans. We are among a handful of towns that can claim this unusual distinction. I came upon this realization about 25 years ago when I took up a lifelong hankering to ride a motorcycle. I made a goal of riding both of those highways from end to end. I was able to accomplish my goal, albeit not all at one time. It was a great way to see this vast country.

But it is not the characteristics of Lexington and Rockbridge County that I am about here. They are only peripheral to my focus on the object of my peculiar attraction – House Mountain.

HOUSE MOUNTAIN ALLURE

What is it about House Mountain that appeals to us? Of course its proximity to and visibility from Lexington make it prominent as does the fact that it is distinctly separate and unto itself. Morton wrote in 1920: "Since the House mountains rise like islands from the floor of the Valley of Virginia their isolation, their lofty summits, and their exceptional form render them a striking feature in a Rockbridge landscape." The mountain is on the eastern edge of the massive Allegheny Mountain range, but it stands alone as an outlier in the Valley. Almost all literature on Lexington, whether historical, descriptive or promotional contains a photograph or painting of it. There are other peaks in Lexington's westerly pantheonic mountain range including Big Butt, Hog Back and Jump, but none have the appeal of the location, size and shape of House. House Mountain conveys beauty, uniqueness, independence, massiveness, antiquity, constancy, immutability, guardianship and even sacredness. Its configuration, individuality, aloofness and its interaction with nature make it unique. It is not only a monument of beauty but a symbol of Divine Nature.

NOT ONE BUT TWO

House Mountain is a misnomer. It should be House Mountains because it is not one but two mountains – Little House Mountain and Big House Mountain, which are joined together at the hip by a saddle of lesser elevation. From the perspective of Lexington or as seen from Interstate 81, Little House Mountain is predominant with Big House Mountain peeking around from behind the southern edge. To the unknowing or undiscerning eye, on most days and in most weather conditions it is difficult to see that one is looking at two separate mountains. Only on close examination and especially from different locations do the two mountains become apparent. It could be said that House Mountain is, indeed, one mountain with two peaks, but that doesn't jibe with its subordinate plural nomenclatures. I do not know if it is the singular appearance of its Lexington oriented face, an historical reason or just common usage that dictates that the House Mountains are referred to as House Mountain.

OTHER ILLUSIONS

Another misperception is that House Mountain is due west from Lexington. Actually, the mountain is north west of the town. We have a tendency to think that the Blue Ridge and Alleghany mountain ranges run due north or due south, depending on whether one is observing as a Southerner or Yankee. To the contrary they run southwesterly to northeasterly at an angle to due north which distorts our directional orientation when looking at the ranges, including our perspective of where House lies in relation to Lexington. The maps on page 31 demonstrates this geographic and geological feature.

Finally, to dispel another related misinterpretation, House Mountain is technically not located in the Shenandoah Valley nor do we citizens of Lexington and Rockbridge County live in that valley. The Shenandoah Valley, a part of the Great Valley of Virginia, encompasses the watershed of the north and south forks of the Shenandoah River. The watershed

Section II: Community Portrait

begins in the southern edge of Augusta County and eastern Bath County and flows into the forks of the Shenandoah north of Staunton, which used to bill itself as the "Queen City of the Shenandoah." From there the two forks run north on either side of the Massanutten Mountain Range between the Blue Ridge Mountains and the Alleghany Range to Front Royal where they join and run to Harper's Ferry and into the Potomac River. We are in the Maury River watershed of the Valley of Virginia where the streams run east and south into the Maury River. The Maury then runs into the James River close to Glasgow. Over the years it has become accepted to say that anyone from Hagerstown to Roanoke lives in the Shenandoah Valley.

The generally accepted notion that Lexington is located in the Shenandoah Valley is in a small way perpetuated among VMI cadets and alumni by the fact that for decades the signature song of the VMI Glee Club has been the much-loved-traditional-folk song, "Shenandoah." I think it is also a staple of the W&L chorus.

One other note: The people of the 18th and 19th centuries would not recognize our contemporary notion that we are going "up" the Valley from Staunton to Harrisonburg or toward Winchester because that is north and therefore up. They would have said that they were going down the Valley because that's the way the main river flows. To the contrary, if we are driving from Lexington to Glasgow, we may well say that we are going down (south) to Glasgow. That would be in keeping with our forbearers because that is the direction the Maury River runs between the two towns. To avoid confusion one must be aware of these changed directional assumptions when reading historical descriptions of the Great Valley.

For reference, on page 32 there is an excellent topographical rendering distributed by the Rockbridge Area Conservation Council which clearly depicts some of my points: the kidney shapes of the two distinct House Mountains which stand as separate from any surrounding mountains, the fact that one is behind the other when viewed from Lexington, the confirmation that House Mountain is west by northwest of Lexington, and that Rockbridge County's Maury River watershed runs south and is part of the James River watershed.

Section II: Community Portrait

HOUSE MOUNTAIN FACTS

The elevations of the two peaks of House Mountain are not high even by Virginia standards. Big House is 3,645 feet high, making it the 184th highest in Virginia and Little House is 3,386 feet, making it the 300th highest in the state. By comparison the highest peak in Virginia is Mount Rogers in Grayson County in Southwest Virginia at 5,722 feet. A second comparison is Mount Washington in New Hampshire at 6,288 feet, making it the highest mountain in the northern Alleghenies. I have climbed Mount Rogers and Mount Washington and both are difficult day climbs, but I do not remember having to go up slopes any steeper than the face of House.

The length at the mesa-like top of Little House is about three-quarters of a mile and that of Big House, although taller, about a quarter of a mile. The saddle between the two mountains can be accessed by a trail going up the southerly end of Little House with a relatively modest incline at which point one can continue on a trail to the top of Big House in about 45 minutes. Such a hike is much less arduous than climbing the face of Little House to the Overlook, the rock outcropping that is plainly visible at the northerly end of Little House and as described in the note on page 4.

The House Mountain saddle, now much overgrown, was once an apple orchard and pasture. Foundations of homesteads both at the saddle and along the trail from below are visible in the underbrush, particularly in the winter. Homesteading in the 19th and early 20th centuries on that remote and inaccessible mountain must have required hardy people. Now the saddle has an open camping shelter that can sleep up to eight hikers side-by-side, other primitive camping sites and a privy.

There is a variety of trees and bushes on the mountains much like what is found in all the Appalachians in the mid Atlantic states. The mountain laurel is a sight to behold when in bloom. The fauna on the mountains is typical of that on any western Virginia mountains: black bears, deer galore, turkeys, some grouse, and maybe an occasional wildcat or coyote. The one large animal no longer seen in the Valley or its contiguous mountains is the woods buffalo, which was prevalent until hunted to extinction in the late 18th and early 19th centuries by the growing population of white men. Reminders of their existence are the names of many local streams such as Buffalo Creek, and the Cowpasture and

Section II: Community Portrait

Bullpasture rivers. The mountain lion and the wolf lasted longer than the buffalo, but are also long gone, although local residents insist there have been recent sightings of mountain lions.

SISTER MOUNTAIN PEAKS

As one surveys from Lexington the beginning of the eastern edge of the Appalachian Range he will note other interesting mountain peaks. Running generally north from House they are Big Butt (3,455 feet), Hog Back (2,538 feet) and Jump (2,451 feet). Each is interesting for its own configuration. Hog Back, a well-known landmark, is known for its catchy name, and Jump could be considered as a signature mountain for the northern part of Rockbridge County. It has been particularly familiar to a number of generations of summer campers at Camp Maxwelton, a boys' camp close to its base. The campers who come from all over the state and beyond remember Jump well because they climb it every year. New campers are awed by the Indian legend about a brave from one tribe and a young squaw from another who fell in love but whose relationship was not condoned by the two tribes. Hand in hand, they jumped to their deaths from the precipice at the northern end of the mountain. There are variations to the story, but its general sense is probably where Jump Mountain got its name.

I have climbed all of these sister mountains and will attest that none comes close to the challenge of climbing House's steep face. Indeed, a good, challenging day hike would be to climb the face of Little House to the Overlook, cross the top of Little House to the Saddle, climb the trail to the top of Big House, backtrack to the saddle and hike down to the parking area at the trailhead. It would require two vehicles as you would start from one location and end up in another. Most of my assaults on the face of House Mountain have been in accomplishing the family climbing ritual described in the Introduction, but I have climbed all the other components separately. On page 33 there is a topographical rendering of the two House Mountains.

In Lexington the sister mountains do not carry the same cachet as House because they are farther away, are not entirely unto themselves, do not give the sense that they preside over the town and are not considered signature landmarks. In the western part of Rockbridge County, people share a similarly possessive sense about House Mountain, although it is seen from very different perspectives. A photo of all of Lexington's peaks is on pages 38-39.

GEOLOGY

The formation of the Appalachian Mountains, and hence House Mountain, goes back almost 500 million years. It is not my intention here to give a detailed history of the complicated eras of radical geological evolution that molded the Appalachian Range into what it is today. Simplistically, there is evidence of thrust and faulted marine sedimentary rocks, plate collisions, submersions under shallow seas and further plate motions. All of this was followed by several cycles of emergence of mountains, erosion, further uplifting and erosions. For a complete analysis of the evolution of the Appalachians, I recommend the U.S. Geological Survey website and for local geology Geology of Rockbridge County shown in section XIII under Wilkes, G.P. et al.

INDIANS

In his book, *Remarkable Rockbridge*, The Story of Rockbridge County, Virginia, Charles A. Bodie states:

> *The earliest people of Rockbridge belonged to a group that scholars have called Indians of the Eastern Woodland. Preceding the earliest Europeans by thousands of years, they lived east of the Great Plains, from Canada to the Gulf of Mexico. Indians were hunting, fishing raising families, and some cases, building large urban settlements along the banks of America's rivers long before Columbus's ships first landed in the West Indies in 1492.*

Bodie indicates that the debate continues over how long the Indians populated North America before the arrival of the Europeans. Indian remains of 11,000 years ago have been found in the northern Valley and of 20,000 years ago in the Piedmont section of Virginia.

Section II: Community Portrait

Parke Rouse Jr., in his book *The Great Wagon Road*, says:

> *The tribes which bounded the Great Warriors' path were almost as diverse as the English farmers, French tradesmen, German protestants, and Scottish lowlanders who were to settle this part of the New World. Each of the tribes belonged to one of four major language groups, or 'nations' which Europeans found living in the woodlands or eastern America in the early year of American colonization.*

The nations were the Iroquorian, Algonquians, Siouans, and Muskhogeans. The primary Indian descendants in Rockbridge County today are of the Monacan tribe of Siouan background. There are about 1,700 living in Virginia and in 1989 the Monacan tribe was recognized by the Virginia General Assembly as one of the eight indigenous tribes in the Commonwealth. The Nation is headquartered in Amherst County and carries on the proud traditions of the tribe. Natural Bridge has a Monacan Living History Village as a teaching and tourist attraction.

I find no information that the Monacans or any Indians had any particular affinity with House Mountain.. One can bet that they were aware of it, but apparently, unlike Natural Bridge, did not revere it. However, local lore holds that they referred to the mountains as the "breasts of the earth."

EXPLORATION

It took over a hundred years from when Jamestown was settled in 1607 for Virginia to reach out publicly beyond the Piedmont. Unquestionably, there had been many previous explorations by adventurers and seekers of Eldorado. Indeed, as reported by William H. Funk in an article, *Return of a Native: The Virginia Elk*, in the November/December 2013 *Virginia Wildlife* magazine:

> *Anno Domini 1666. While across the ocean the Great Fire was leveling the wooden London of Chaucer and Shakespeare, that city's Royal representative, Sir William Berkeley, His Majesty's Governor of the sprawling Colony of Virginia dispatched a reconnaissance team of 14 settlers guided by 14 Natives to survey the unknown territory beyond the thickly wooded*

Section II: Community Portrait

Blue Ridge Mountains, then fully ablaze in the splendor of autumn. Sixty years before Alexander Spotswood and his fabled Knights of the Golden Horseshoe crossed over Swift Run Rap these initial agents of the Crown descended the steep western slopes and beheld and Edenic panorama: a verdant valley laced with rushing waterways, cradled on the far side but a still greater mountain range and stretching away to the northeast and southwest as far as their eyes could follow.

Already the explorers could see that this lovely vale was home to plentiful wildlife with droves of mighty herbivores ranging the valley floor. Deer browsed the riparian in tree line and immense shaggy wood bison grazed on lush bunches of switchgrass and big bluestem. A sharp-eyed Indian pointed out a pack of wolves lazing in the sunshine beside a gnawed deer carcass. A bear drinking from a riverbank raised its head to glance curiously at the visitors, muzzle dripping. As the Englishman stared hungrily at the fertile fields before them, doubtless imagining stately plantations supplanting the wildlife, they heard from somewhere below a strange whistling shriek like a coughing scream that bounced off the mountain bluffs and ricocheted down the valley.... The natives smiled at this misplaced fear and, gathering their bows, led the team downward in the direction of the first crier. They knew well the mating call of the wapiti and that it meant for them it was time to hunt…

As Funk indicated, it was not until 1716, (50 years after Funk's account – contrary to his stated 60 years) that the story later to appear in the history books unfolded. Governor Alexander Spotswood and a caravan of 63 men, to be later dubbed by the governor as "The Knights of the Golden Horseshoe," breached the Blue Ridge Mountains at Swift Run Gap and discovered the beauty and assets of the Great Valley.

They knew how to celebrate their success! Parke Rouse quotes from a diary composed by an Ensign John Fontaine, who was among the explorers:

We had a good dinner and after we got the men together, and loaded all their arms, and we drank the King's health in champagne, and fired a volley – the Princess's health in burgundy, and fired a volley, and all the rest of the Royal Family on claret, and a volley. We drank the governor's health and fired another volley. We had several sorts of liquors, viz. Virginia red wine and white wine, Irish usquebaugh brandy shrub, two sorts of rum, champagne, canary, cherry, punch, water, cider &c.

Section II: Community Portrait

Although the partying places some doubt on the exploratory validity of the Governor's group, he seemed, like all politicians throughout history, to be good at public relations. There is little wonder why from that point on there was no stopping the vast migration west and south into the Valley and beyond.

However, it still took decades for the valley to become mostly civilized. As noted by Dan Guzy in an essay in Volume 122 of the *Virginia Magazine* of The Virginia Historical Society:

> *In December 1742, while Lord Fairfax was back in England defending his proposed proprietary boundaries, a skirmish between European settlers and Iroquois passing through the Shenandoah Valley resulted in the deaths of ten whites and four Indians. This increased tensions and made the land beyond the Blue Ridge temporarily less desirable. The Virginia government, however, negotiated the Treaty of Lancaster (1744) by which the Iroquois agreed to give up their claim to the Shenandoah Valley and avoid contact with settlers. Thus, for a while, the rich land in that valley and to the west could be settled more peacefully….*
>
> *With the final mapping of the Fairfax Grant in 1747, the Shenandoah Valley rapidly grew in population. The French and Indian and Pontiac wars temporarily halted this growth, but within only a few decades, the settlement of the Valley would serve as a model for regions farther west, like Kentucky. As historian Warren R. Hostra noted, the backcountry soon became the forecountry….*

The earliest written reference to House Mountain that I can find is in Volume I of Colonel William Couper's *History of the Shenandoah Valley*:

> *And so it was probable before 1757 that a road ran between Purgatory Mountain and the Short Hills, through Cartmill's Gap which swung over to the west side of the Valley and proceeded northward by way of 'Courthouse Staunton.'… There it is called 'The Great Road…" On this map there is a prominent bulge toward the Alleghenies, apparently near Goshen Pass, but this road in hugging the foothills of the mountains passed around the two House Mountains …."*

Section II: Community Portrait

So the House Mountains were identified as such as early as 1757 and it is interesting to note that they were then referred to in the plural.

PATHWAY OF THE GREAT VALLEY

The Cherokee tribe of the Iroquoians and the Shawnee tribe of the Algonquians dominated the Great Warriors Path, the ancient Indian trail that extended the entire length of the Great Valley of Virginia. The Great Warriors Path morphed into the Great Philadelphia Wagon Road that carried the masses of European settlers who arrived in Philadelphia and moved on to settle in the Valley. Some later pushed farther West and South, settling in what is now West Virginia, Ohio, Tennessee, North Carolina and South Carolina. Except for New England, the Great Wagon Road was truly the umbilical cord from Europe to America.

The Great Wagon Road later morphed into the "Valley Pike," which was its primary road, providing a route for troop movements during battles in the Valley during the Civil War, especially Stonewall Jackson's famous Valley Campaign. Then around the turn of the 20th century the Valley Pike became U. S. Route 11 and continued to fulfill its role as the main highway artery running the length of the Valley, only now it was carrying motorized vehicles. Since humans have occupied the Valley, this route has changed from a footpath to a dirt road, to partially wooden planks (Rockbridge still has a road named Plank Road.) to gravel, to paved highway and to super highway. It is a good bet that each step of this progress has brought on nostalgic feelings and a sense of loss.

SAVING HOUSE MOUNTAIN

In 1988, a large part of House Mountain that was visible to Lexington, including the two peaks and the saddle, came on the market. Consisting of 900 plus acres, it had been owned by David White for twenty years and was priced at $325,000. Concerned that the property could be purchased for development, thereby destroying its scenic and historical value, the community came together to take action. After some months of consultation with local state officials and organizations,

Section II: Community Portrait

the Rockbridge Area Conservation Council (RACC) explored the possibility of acquiring and preserving the Mountain. A fundraising committee was formed on which I was privileged to serve, and an intensive campaign was conducted to solicit funds from individuals, corporations and foundations. The two colleges granted permission to solicit their alumni. RACC acquired an option to purchase the mountain, then partnered with the Virginia Outdoor Foundation (VOF), which contributed the remaining funds needed to complete the purchase. RACC conveyed its option to VOF which took title to the property

VOF is a state authorized foundation, which owns natural preserves and private conservation easements in the Commonwealth. Management of the Mountain is under the joint auspices of RACC, and the VOF, which formed a committee for that specific purpose. Again, I had the pleasure of serving on that committee for its first few years. Its mission is to preserve the natural character of the mountain by limiting timbering, vehicle access and use only for hikers, campers and hunters. At this writing certain management differences between RACC and VOF have arisen, even after twenty-five years of a successful partnership. It is hoped that they will be worked out to the mutual satisfaction of both parties.

Having been bred amongst mountains
I am always unhappy when in a flat country.
Whenever the skirts of the horizon come on a level with myself
I feel myself quite uneasy and generally have a headache.
(Letter to Sir Walter Scott, 25 July 1802)

James Hogg

Section II: Community Portrait

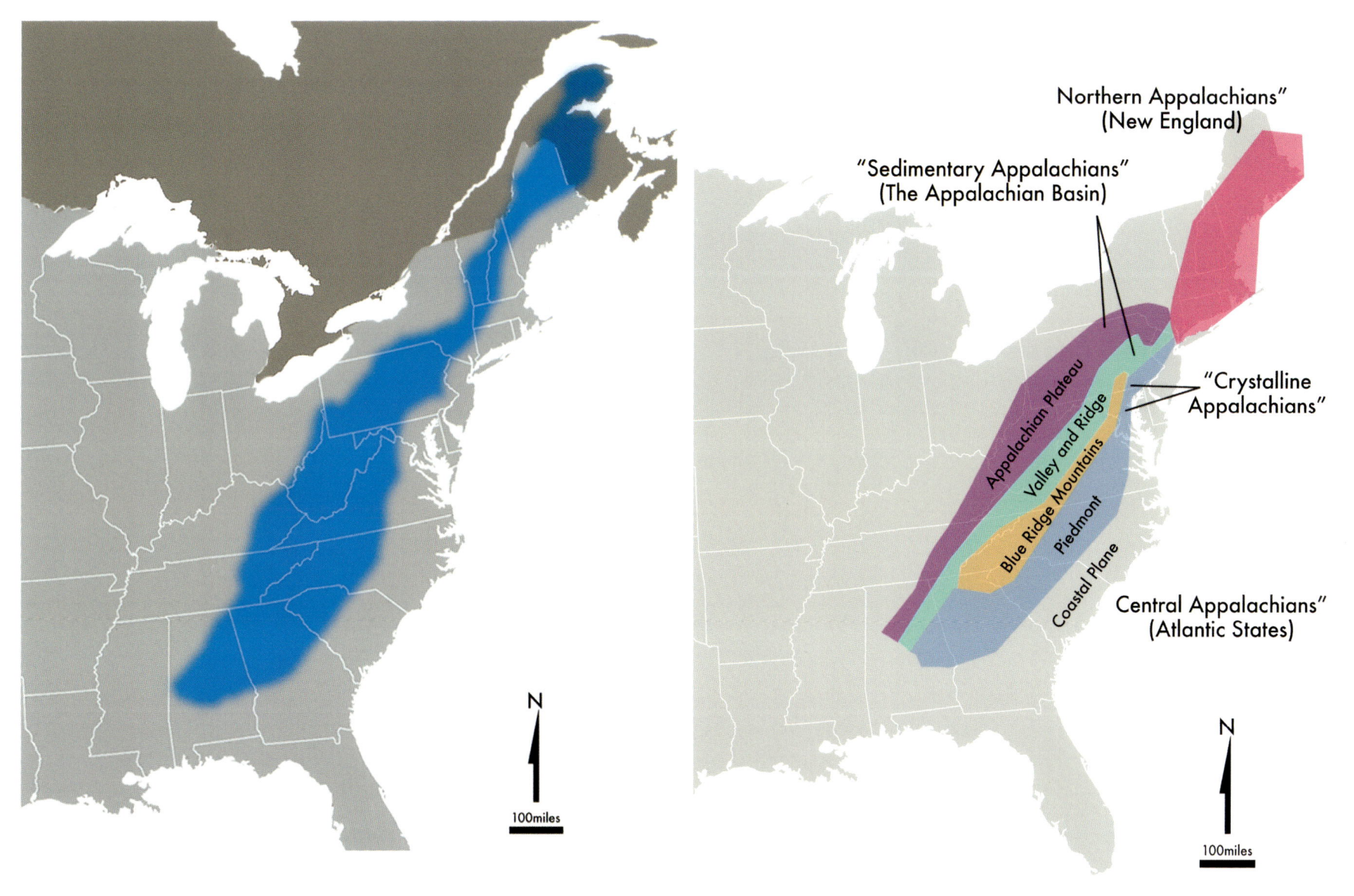

Outline of Appalachian Mountain Range

From the Coast to the Appalachians

Images from Wikipedia

31

Section II: Community Portrait

Topographic Rendering with the Kidney-Shaped House Mountain Visible Five Miles West by Northwest of Lexington

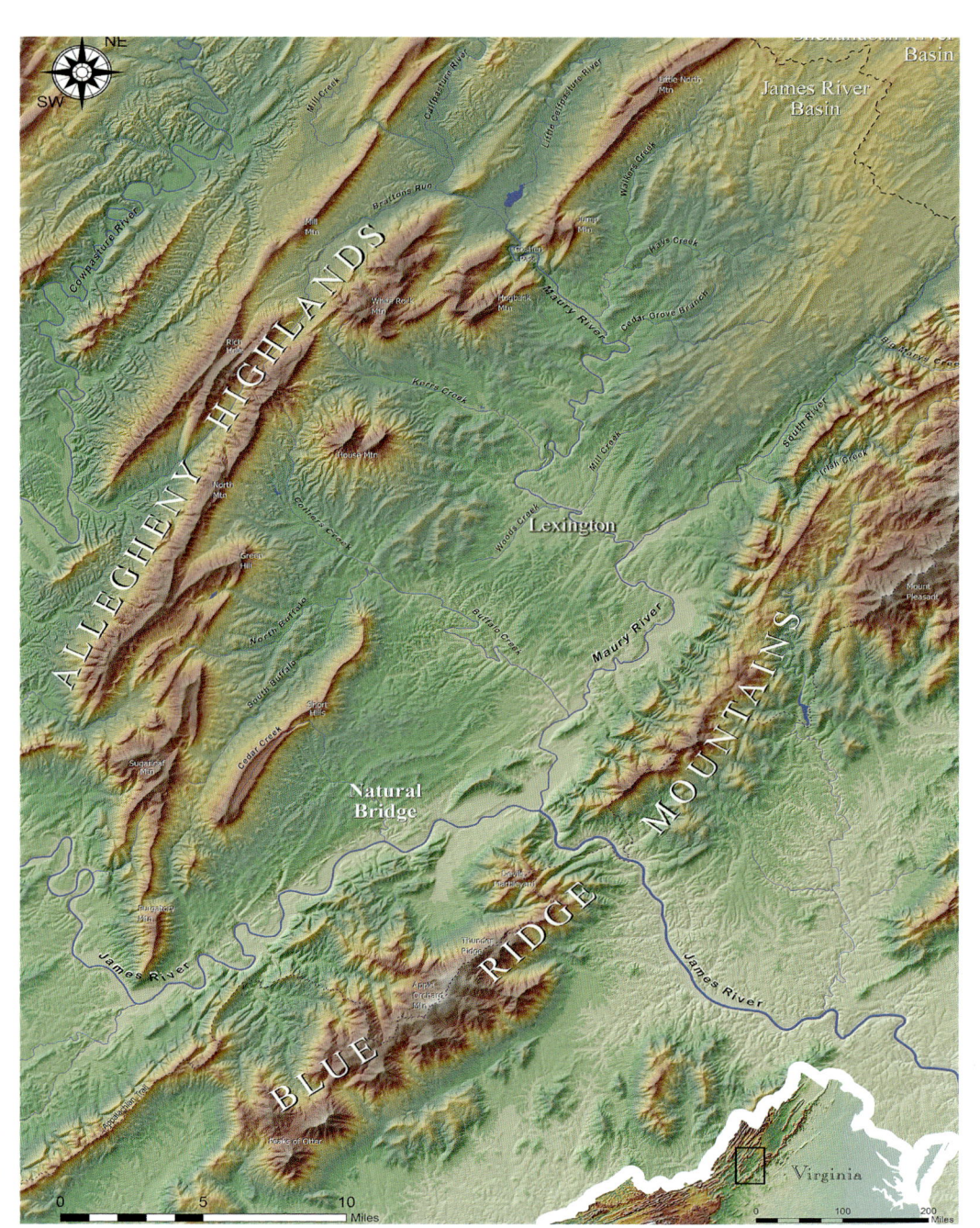

Map from the Rockbridge Area Conservation Council

Section II: Community Portrait

Topographical Rendering of House Mountain Showing Lexington in Top Right

Section II: Community Portrait

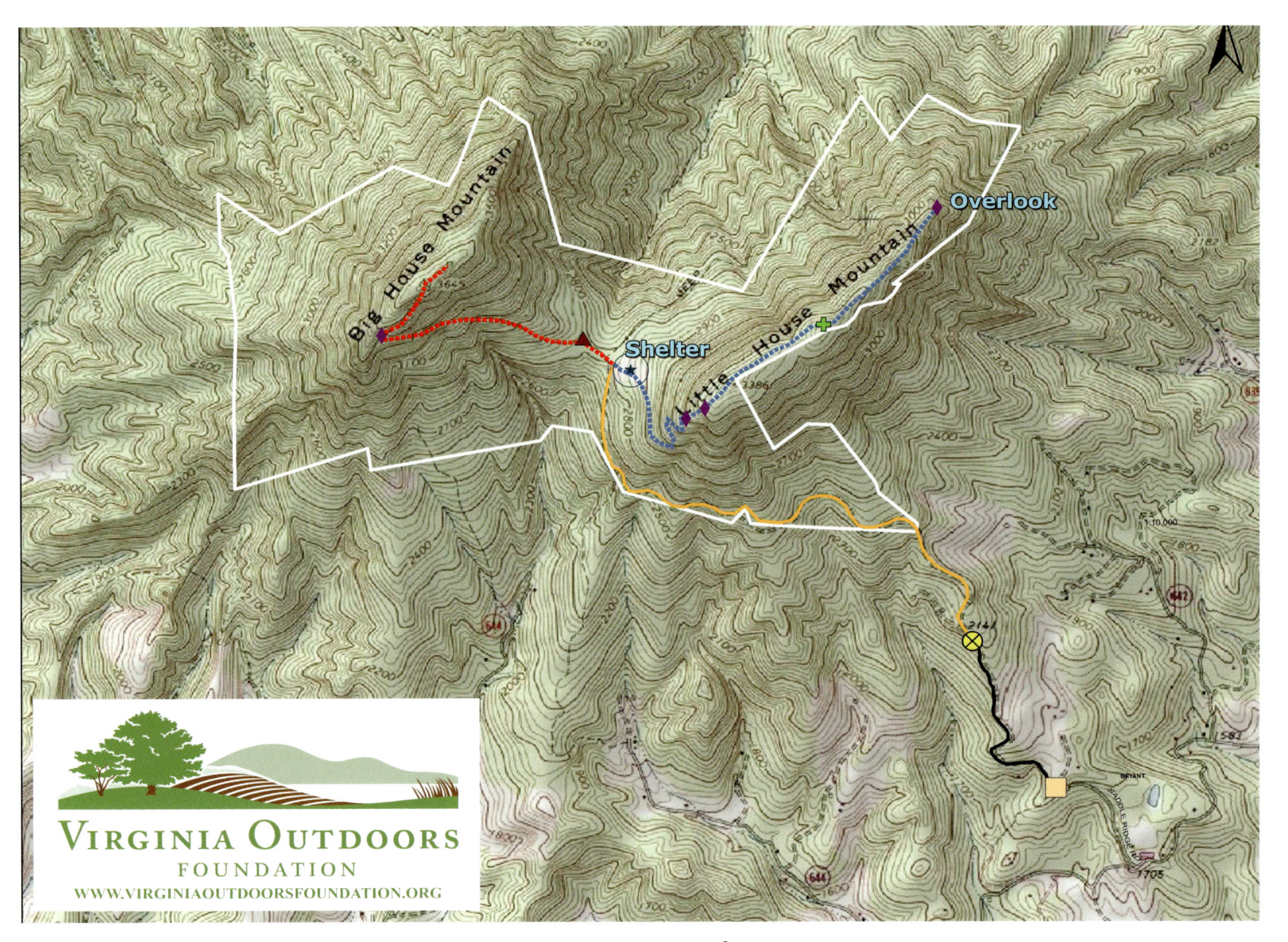

House Mountain Trail Map

Section II: Community Portrait

Rockbridge County's Unique Geological Features

Image from http://en.wikipedia.org/wiki/Natural_Bridge_%28Virginia%29

Natural Bridge
Frederic Edwin Church 1852

Devils Marble Yard
Image from http://virginiatrailguide.com/2012/05/13/the-devils-marbleyard/

35

Section II: Community Portrait

The Lexington Look - Summer

Section II: Community Portrait

The Lexington Look - Winter

Section II: Community Portrait

Lexington's Mountain Peaks:

House   Big Butt

Photo by Cabell Gorman

Section II: Community Portrait

Lexington's Mountain Peaks:

Hogback   Jump

Section II: Community Portrait

Jump Mountain in Northern Rockbridge County

Jump Mountain Peak from Camp Maxwelton

Section III
Transfiguration by Circumnavigation

On occasion I have driven with one of my children, grandchildren or another unsuspecting passenger from Lexington west on Interstate 64 toward the Goshen exit and have pointed out House Mountain, prominently visible to the left. "That's not House Mountain!" is the usual response. But this is a classic case of what you think you see is not what you get. Indeed, if you didn't know, you would think that you are viewing two entirely different mountains because they are the antithesis of the appearance of House from Lexington. But, you are looking at a different perspective of both Little House and Big House. Indeed, the look of the two mountains of House Mountain is very different from every vantage point around its entire circumference. For this exercise I will refer to the Mountain in the plural.

To demonstrate this marvel, my wife and I drove for a half-day the full 360 degrees counter-clock-wise around the two mountains to take pictures. It was on a gorgeous spring day, possibly one of the last cool and clear ones before the summer heat and haze began to arrive. On the map (page 42,) on which the two House Mountains are circled in red, one can track our circumferential route in yellow.

> *Mountains, according to the angle of view, the season, the time of day, the beholder's frame of mind, or any one thing, can effectively change their appearance. Thus, it is essential to recognize that we can never know more than one side, one small aspect of a mountain.*
>
> Haruki Murakami, *A Wild Sheep Chase*

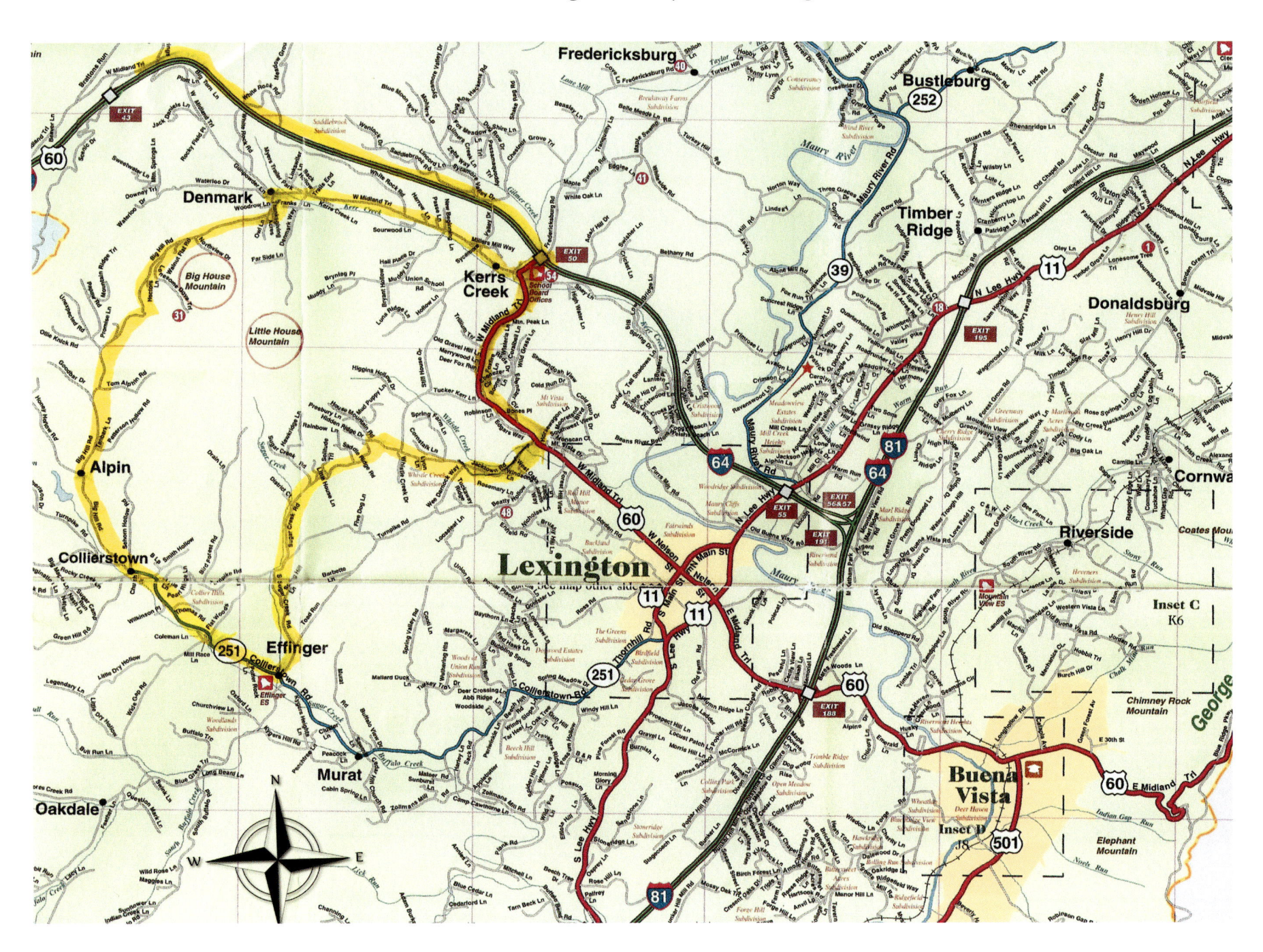

Section III: Transfiguration by Circumnavigation

42

Section III: Transfiguration by Circumnavigation

The Transfiguration Begins
The Front of the Overlook of Little House on the Left, and the Appearance of Big House on the Right
Photo Taken From Kerrs Creek East of the Mountains

Section III: Transfiguration by Circumnavigation

Little House on the Left Showing its Length and Mesa-Like Top Contrasted to the Rounded Top of Big House
Photo Taken from I-64 Almost Due North of House Mountains

Section III: Transfiguration by Circumnavigation

Big House Blocks Little House
Photo Taken East of Denmark Due North of the Mountains

Section III: Transfiguration by Circumnavigation

The Two Mountains Come Back into View with the Saddle in the Middle and Big House Predominant on the Left
Photo Taken Near Collierstown Southwest of the Mountains

Section III: Transfiguration by Circumnavigation

The Overlook on Little House (Right) and its Reciprocal Precipice on Big House (Left) Come into View
Photo Taken Near Effinger South of the Mountains

Section III: Transfiguration by Circumnavigation

The Side of Big House Over the Saddle Becomes Clear
Photo From Due South of the Mountains

Section III: Transfiguration by Circumnavigation

Around the Horn – the Face of Little House Looms and the Saddle Recedes
Photo Taken East of Effinger and South of the Mountains

Section III: Transfiguration by Circumnavigation

Circumnavigation Complete
Return to the Familiar Face of the Little House with Edge of Big House Visible on the Left
Photo Taken from Southeast of the Mountains

Section IV
Spiritual Connotations

RELIGIONS AND MOUNTAINS

Since the beginning of humanity mountains have been associated with spiritual experiences. The ancients assumed that the tops of mountains were, by definition, closer to where the gods existed. Norse, Greek and Iranian mythologies considered that mountains were the actual seats of the gods. Mount Olympus in Greece was the mythological home of the twelve Greek gods and was described this way by Homer: "Olympus was not shaken by winds nor ever wet with rain, nor did snow fall upon it, but the air is outspread clear and cloudless, and over it hovered a radiant whiteness."

In the Moslem Quran, quotations about mountains seem almost more tangible and worldly than spiritual: "We placed firmly embedded mountains in the earth so it would not move under them…." (Quran 21:31) "Have we not made the earth as a bed, and the mountains as pegs?" (Quran 78:6-7) Islamists consider it a marvel that these statements conveying the stabilizing effect of mountains on the crust of the earth were written centuries before their claim that it is now a geological fact. Mountains are closely associated with Hinduism, which is composed of many sects and doctrines that influence life in India. The Himalayas occupy an important place in Hindu mythology as their summits represent the heavens. The mountains are the home of holy men - the yogis and sadhus (ascetic wandering monks) who live in ding (focused) meditation. Buddhism is a nominal religion because there is no worship of an omniscient god, but is a belief in various practices and teachings of Buddha, meaning "the awakened one," who lived and taught in the Indian/Tibetan area between the 6th and 4th centuries, BC. Because the teachings of Buddhism focus on the internal primacy of the mind, there is less emphasis on external features like mountains.

BIBLICAL MOUNTAINS

Judaism and Christianity possibly above all the religions emphasize the symbolism of mountains. *Strong's Exhaustive Concordance of the Bible* lists some 575 references to "mount," "mountain," or "mountains" between the Old and New Testaments.

Section IV: Spiritual Connotations

Some of the notable New Testament references to a mountain are Christ's temptation by the devil (Matthew 4:8), the Sermon on the Mount (Matthew 5:1), the admonition that faith can move mountains (Matthew 17:20), the prophetic every mountain and hill being laid low to prepare the way for the Lord (Luke 3:4&5) and the Mount of Olives, the location of the Garden of Gethsemane where Jesus was betrayed (Matthew 26:30).

My favorite unorthodox Christian guru is Emmet Fox who in *Around the Year with Emmet Fox*, said, "The mountain means prayer – elevated consciousness." Many passages of the Bible reflect this if interpreted properly. For example:

> *On Horeb, the mount of God, (another name for Mount Sinai) Elijah came to a cave, and lodged there; and behold the word the Lord came to him…. And he said, 'Go forth, and stand upon the mount of the Lord.'" (I Kings 19: 9-11)*
> *"After six days Jesus took with him Peter and James and John, and led them up a high mountain apart by themselves; and he was transfigured…." (Mark 9:2-3)*
> *"….This is my Son, my beloved, with whom I am well pleased.' We ourselves heard this voice from heaven while we were with him on the holy mountain." (2 Peter 1:16-18)*

The Old Testament is rife with images of mountains such as Mount Ararat where Noah is said to have landed the ark. Perhaps, however, the most widely known and appealing Biblical description of a mountain in the Old Testament is Mount Sinai where Moses, at least metaphorically, went up for his one-on-one meetings with God to receive the Ten Commandments. As a child learning about this story in Sunday school I developed an image of what Mount Sinai looked like. Behold! As depicted on following pages, House Mountain under certain conditions could play the role, maybe even better than the depictions out of artists' minds. However, the contemporary photograph of Mount Sinai on page 56 casts doubts altogether on the traditional perceptions.

RARE RELIGIOUS ACCORD

Interestingly there is one mountain in the world that the four major religions consider a sacred site. It is Sri Pada or Adam's Peak in Sri Lanka. At the 7,359 foot summit there is a five foot long depression in the bedrock like a giant footprint.

Section IV: Spiritual Connotations

To Christians and Moslems it was created by Adam. To Hindus Shia made it. Buddhists believe that it is one of the many traces of Buddha in Asia. It has been famous particularly since Marco Polo wrote about it in the 14th century, and now thousands of pilgrims and tourists of all faiths climb it every year.

LEXINGTON'S SPIRITUAL MOUNTAIN

Whether House Mountain is holy or not, it, along with our other surrounding mountains, plays a symbolic role in the community's religious life. I bet more than half of the local funerals I attend, regardless of what church or funeral home at which they are held, include a reading of Psalm 121. The first verse is, "I will lift mine eyes unto the hills, from whence cometh my help." (St. James's version). Some Bible versions have the Psalm's opening verse followed by a question mark, which may put a slightly different slant on its spiritual interpretation, but it is not my purpose to analyze that here.

The frequent use of Psalm 121 is recognition of the spiritually comforting aspect of living in a valley surrounded by beautiful mountains, the most recognizable and prominent of which for us is House.

Come, let us go up to the mountain of the Lord, to the house of the God of Jacob;
That he may teach us his ways and we may walk in his paths.

Isaiah 2:3

My Father considered a walk among the mountains equivalent to churchgoing.

Aldous Huxley

Section IV: Spiritual Connotations

Artists' Concepts of Mount Sinai where Moses Received the Ten Commandments

Image from http://www.hymntime.com/tch/htm/a/w/a/awakedby.htm *http://www.institutodeltemplo.org/linea_de_tiempo.htm*

Section IV: Spiritual Connotations

House Mountain
Is Moses Up There?
Photo by Michael Ormrod

Section IV: Spiritual Connotations

The Real Mount Sinai

Photo from http://commons.wikimedia.org/wiki/File:Mount_Sinai_Egypt.jpg

Section V
Fanciful Facsimiles

Inasmuch that I have carried on my affair with House Mountain for the better part of a lifetime, I have from time to time in its course, like in all affairs, been reminded of the object of my affection by being attracted to resemblances to it. In each case the resemblance was remote, but interesting in its own right. It speaks volumes as to how easily I reverted to a brief recollection of "my" mountain when I saw them.

I have had a close friendship with Dick Skutt since we both came to Lexington in 1978 – he to teach in the Electrical Engineering Department at VMI and I to run the VMI Foundation. Since neither of our wives had yet joined us, being busy with changing residences, we began to play racquetball regularly and thirty-seven years later we are still at it. We discovered that we had other things in common including relishing outdoor excursions, having a common interest in discussing almost any subject and drinking a few beers, particularly around a campfire. Our compatibility lead over the years to many "old men's adventures" including camping, canoe trips, canoe racing, hiking, tracking the Lewis and Clark Trail across the country, driving 2,100 miles from Canada to Mexico on the Continental Divide on a trail designed for bicycles, skydiving and most recently completing a day hike up Big House Mountain.

It was on the Lewis and Clark trip that an unexpected sighting triggered thoughts about House Mountain. The following is extracted from a journal I kept on the trip:

House Mountain
North Dakota Version
Fort Berthold Indian Reservation
About 11:30 am Sunday, 26 Aug. 2001

I was driving the car on North Dakota Route 23 north when I saw a mesa to the left front that was shaped like House Mountain. I figured I wouldn't say anything to Dick unless we ran into an intersecting road that would take us over there. Sure enough we hit

Section V: Fanciful Facsimiles

McKenzie County Rd. #12 and the mountain was about 2 miles to the west. Road was gravel. I told Dick I had to take a detour for pictures. It was a mesa or butte similarly formed as House Mountain. It also had a small mountain attached, but in this case the smaller one was in the rear of the larger one from our perspective. It has a "student rock" on the right (a misnomer for the Little House Overlook,) but the left end is unlike House. Like House where the Allegheny's begin behind it, the mesa had range of mesas almost out of sight behind it. Therefore, like House, it appeared to be a distinct land elevation unlike anything else around it. The big difference was that, unlike House, which has Lexington 3-4 miles to the east, this mesa had nothing but 2 or 3 ranches in the distance. One probably could see 40 miles from its top. I took some pictures. This may be an interesting comparison for my Peniel Farm/House Mountain study.

On a trip to Israel and Jordan sponsored by Washington and Lee in 2011, I experienced a second and even a quirkier and farfetched example of a mountain slightly resembling House. It was a fascinating trip and one of many highlights was a visit to Masada, a mountain in the desert of Israel near the Dead Sea. It is fascinating because of its history and construction that all but comes alive when touring the site.

House Mountain West

Photo by Dick Skutt

Section V: Fanciful Facsimiles

The use of Masada as a fortress goes back to ancient times, but it was Herod the Great (father of the infamous Herod who was forcefully criticized by John the Baptist for marrying his brother's wife as related in the New Testament Gospels) who really developed the top of the mountain. Herod was the king of Judea from 37 BC to 4 BC and chose Masada to build a luxurious winter palace and fortress. He was a significant builder of his time, also constructing the city of Caesarea on the Mediterranean Sea between 22 and 10 BC and naming it for Caesar Augustus. We also visited the interesting and well-preserved ruins of this city with its enormous port. One fascinating detail was the swimming pool that Herod had carved in the rocks at the edge of the Mediterranean in front of his palace.

Masada's fame was clinched in history when in the Jewish Great Revolt against the Romans, the last surviving rebels fled to Masada in 70 AD. A Roman legion of 8,000 soldiers laid siege, ultimately building a road up the side of the mountain and using a battering ram to destroy the wall. When the hope of the Jewish rebels was at an end, all 960 of them and their families chose to take their own lives rather than to live in shame as Roman slaves.

The fall of Masada was the end of the Jewish uprising and the Romans occupied the site until the beginning of the second century AD.

> *Climb the mountains and get their good tidings. Nature's peace will flow into you as sunshine flows into trees.*
> *The winds will blow their own freshness into you, and the storms their energy,*
> *while cares will drop away from you like the leaves of Autumn.*
>
> John Muir, *The Mountains of California*

Section V: Fanciful Facsimiles

Israeli Answer to House Mountain?
Photo from http://www.israelsir.com/enb/article/draft-on-2013-04-12-19-30-29

Section VI
Sunrises

As seen from Peniel Farm, there are often gorgeous sunrises over the Blue Ridge Mountains. It is exhilarating to then turn around and see the rays from the rising sun strike House Mountain before gradually illuminating the Valley.

The following two photos depict this phenomenon. Note that in the second photo, Big House is clearly visible to the left of Little House, there is snow and the fading moon is beginning to set. The third photo is a winter-rising sun from a different perspective.

We are in the world where the longing mountains are the most grounded.

Sorin Cerin, *Wisdom Collection: The Book of Wisdom*

Section VI: Sunrises

A Blue Ridge Beautiful Morning Glory

Section VI: Sunrises

The Moon Recedes as Sun Begins to Shine on House Mountain

Section VI: Sunrises

Winter Sunrise

Photo by Michele Fletcher

Section VII
Sunsets

The following five pages present three sunsets of resplendent grandure, a sequence of the sun setting southwest of House Mountain and a sunset with overhanging angry clouds.

For all that may be known by men lies plain before their eyes; indeed God himself has disclosed it to them. His invisible attributes, that is to say his everlasting power and deity, have been visible, ever sense the world began, to the eye of reason in the things that he made.

        Romans 1: 19-20
        New Testament
        The New English Bible

        Like a god going thro' his world
        There stands one mountain,
        For a moment in the dusk,
        Whole brotherhoods of cedars are its brow.

        Robert Browning

Section VII: Sunsets

Section VII: Sunsets

Section VII: Sunsets

Section VII: Sunsets

69

Section VIII: Clouds

Section VIII: Clouds

Section VIII: Clouds

Section IX
Moons

Predicting the trajectory of the moon for me is neither a science nor an art. It seems irrationally to change from night to night, and I count it as a matter of pure luck to catch it on a clear night setting over House Mountain. Following are examples of those rare occasions:

> *The moon is a loyal companion.*
> *It never leaves. It's always there, watching, steadfast, knowing us in our light and dark moments,*
> *changing forever just as we do. Every day it's a different version of itself. Sometimes weak and wan,*
> *sometimes strong and full of light. The moon understands what it means to be human.*
> *Uncertain. Alone. Cratered by imperfections."*

Tahereh Mafi, *Shatter Me*

Section IX: Moons

Winter Conjunction Over House Mountain
The Moon, Venus and Barely-Visible Jupiter
Photo by Michele Fletcher

76

Section IX: Moons

The Moon Sets Over the Little House Overlook

Section IX: Moons

Birds Bear Witness to the Retreating Moon, Which Chooses to Set on the Side of Big House Mountain

78

Section X
Four Seasons

Spring, if it lingers more than a week beyond its span, starts to hunger for summer to end the days of perpetual promise. Summer in its turn soon begins to sweat for something to quench its heat, and the mellowest of autumns will tire of gentility at last, and ache for a quick sharp frost to kill its fruitfulness. Even winter — the hardest season, the most implacable — dreams, as February creeps on, of the flame that will presently melt it away. Everything tires with time, and starts to seek some opposition, to save it from itself.

Clive Barker, *The Hellbound Heart*

All Photographs in this Section by R. Amanda Loreti

Section X: Four Seasons

Spring

Section X: Four Seasons

Summer

Section X: Four Seasons

Autumn

Section X: Four Seasons

Winter

Section X: Four Seasons

This is June, the month of grass and leaves… already the aspens are trembling again, and a new summer is offered me. I feel a little fluttered in my thoughts, as if I might be too late. Each season is but an infinitesimal point. It no sooner comes than it is gone. It has no duration. It simply gives a tone and hue to my thought. Each annual phenomena is reminiscence and prompting. Our thoughts and sentiments answer to the revolution of the seasons, as two cog-wheels fit into each other. We are conversant with only one point of contact at a time, from which we receive a prompting and impulse and instantly pass to a new season or point of contact. A year is made up of a certain series and number of sensations and thoughts which have their language in nature. Now I am ice, now I am sorrel. Each experience reduces itself to a mood of the mind.

Henry David Thoreau, Journal, June 6, 1857

Section XI
Notable Scenes and Items

Following is a final potpourri of unusual photographs, paintings and items pertaining to House Mountain.

A Stained Glass Rendering of Lexington's Two Prominent Natural Assets: the Maury River and House Mountain

Section XI: Notable Scenes and Items

Michael Miley (1841 - 1918)

After the surrender, there came to the community an ex-Confederate soldier and an artist of unusual ability, Mike Miley, who perpetuated the picture business. Miley's contribution to the world was great. To him is due the credit for many of the best photographic studies of General Lee. Wherever these photographs have gone, has also gone - 'Photo by Miley'.

Henry Boley, *Lexington in Old Virginia*

House Mountain as Background to Washington an Lee University

The Michael Miley Collection, Special Collections and Archives, Washington and Lee University

Section XI: Notable Scenes and Items

House Mountain on Far Right as Seen from Warm Springs Mountain 20 Miles Northwest of Lexington
Photo by R. Amanda Loreti

Section XI: Notable Scenes and Items

An Osprey, Tilt-Rotor Aircraft Buzzes Over House Mountain
Photo by Mike Ormrod

Section XI: Notable Scenes and Items

Another House Mountain Affair (Anne Drake, circa 1952)

Section XI: Notable Scenes and Items

An Exceptional Photo from a July 4th Balloon Rally Sponsored by the Lexington Rotary Club Foundation
Photo by Michele Fletcher

Section XI: Notable Scenes and Items

Section XI: Notable Scenes and Items

19th Century Lithograph of House Mountain Overlooking VMI

Section XI: Notable Scenes and Items

Painting by Noted Local Artist, Maxine Foster, 1990, on the Occasion of the House Warming at Peniel Farm

Section XI: Notable Scenes and Items

New Cadets Climb House Mountain as Part of Matriculation Week Activities
Photo courtesy of VMI Communications & Marketing

Section XI: Notable Scenes and Items

House Mountain Volcano

Photo by Mike Ormrod

Section XI: Notable Scenes and Items

House Mountain

In the Shenandoah county
Is an old Virginia town—
Full of legend and history
Full of romance and renown

With the Blue Ridge for a background—
Sometimes green, then with blue with haze—
There we find in stately dignity
The homes of old Virginia days.

There's an atmosphere and essence
To these homes of long ago
That brings to mind the mountain roads
'Long which the laurels grow.

And the steeps of rhododendron
Which no artist can portray
And the banks of honey suckle
Which blankets all the way.

And ever in the background
Looms House Mountain—dim or clear
There it's stood in magic stateliness
For lo! This many a year.

With its top well mossed with
Groups of trees
It's side with patches bare.
Sometimes glittering in sunshine
Sometimes shadows here and there.

Sometimes it has a night cap on,
Sometimes a gauzy gown.
Sometimes it shows a face of smiles,
Sometimes it seems to frown.

Skies, sometimes, blue above it,
Sometimes hedged in white or grey.
There's no argument of beauty
Tho' it changes from day to day.

'tis a masterpiece of workmanship
And when evening drops down cool
I like to think god's resting there
With House Mountain as his foot stool.

By Mary Hamilton Ingersoll, Elyria, Ohio
Written from VMI parade ground in late 19th
or early 20th Century
Archives, Washington and Lee University

Section XI: Notable Scenes and Items

Author Viewing "Back Side" of Little House Over the Saddle from Big House
Photo by Dick Skutt

Section XI: Notable Scenes and Items

The Seal of Lexington Commemorating its 1966 Designation as a City, and portraying a Lamp of Learning Symbolizing its Two Colleges and House Mountain, its Iconic Landmark

Section XII
Epilogue

A SON OF THE VALLEY

It has dawned on me in the course of producing this book that House Mountain is symbolic of a personal geographic affinity of greater scope than just the mountain itself. I am a product of the South as modified by Virginia as modified by the Valley of Virginia as symbolized by House Mountain. I have lived in the Valley for 55 years, although not consecutively. It had a profound effect on my youth and continues to attract me as well as Sis as our chosen place on earth.

VALLEY ROOTS

I was born and grew up in Staunton, which in the 1940's and '50's was a Valley-small-town heaven and a haven for children and teenagers. I was fortunate to witness the end of the Great Depression and experience the heartache and victory of World War II. My father, who had long been in the Army National Guard, spent almost a year on active duty before the war and four years in England and Europe during the war. Despite my father's absence and the threat of polio, a frightening children's disease in those days that kept us home bound in the summers, I recall it as a halcyon time. I had an older brother and many neighborhood friends with whom to pal around. We had the facilities of the Staunton Military Academy (long defunct and now part of Mary Baldwin College) almost in our backyard and all but lived on its athletic fields. I have often told Sis that the world peaked in 1947 when I turned twelve. I felt I was a junior master of the world. Life was grand and it was the BG era – Before Girls.

Robert E. Lee High School was the quintessential small high school of the late '40's and '50's. When speaking at the funeral of one of my childhood friends several years ago I said of our youth, "If the TV sitcom 'Happy Days,' was not modeled on Staunton it should have been." There was simplicity of life that reflected the times and culture of the town.

Section XII: Epilogue

Dad had acquired in the 1930's a rustic family camp in the foothills of the Alleghany Mountains west of Churchville and Buffalo Gap, 13 miles from Staunton. From an early age it gave me an appreciation for the mountainous wilderness bordering the Valley, formed my appreciation of nature, and served as an escape and hunting place well into my adulthood. In the summers of '48 and '49, I went to Boy Scout camp at Camp Shenandoah when it was located on the South Fork of the Shenandoah River near McGayhesville. The next summer I attended the newly relocated camp near Swoope, and then in 1951 I became a counselor and drove the camp truck, which required me to learn a lot about the highways and by-ways of the Great Valley.

I attended Episcopal High School in Alexandria from 1951 to 1953, taking me away from the Valley for the first time, but the experience at the school was indelible. In 1952 I was, at the invitation of Lee McLaughlin, the EHS and later W&L football coach, a counselor at Camp Maxwelton near Brownsburg. His son now runs the camp at its present location under Jump Mountain, and I have three grandsons attending and one graduate of seven camp seasons.

In the summer of 1953, I worked as a bus boy in the old gate house at Natural Bridge. I lived in the back of the old hotel. It was a real coming of age experience. That fall I entered VMI and for four years claimed Lexington as my residence and got to know the town, albeit most of my time was spent at the Institute where I began my affair with House Mountain.

One of my most memorable Valley experiences was in the summer of 1954 when one of my friends, Tommy Simmons, and I packed up an old borrowed canvas canoe. Departing from Weyers Cave north of Staunton, we canoed 300 miles down North River to the South Fork of the Shenandoah River to Front Royal and the Big Shenandoah River to Harper's Ferry and the Potomac River and ended up in front of the Lincoln Memorial in Washington. We portaged nine dams, and on the Potomac northwest of Washington ran the Great Falls with no knowledge of their difficulty and danger, turning over frequently. Today running the Great Falls is considered extremely dangerous and is only for experienced kayakers. We were lucky we didn't drown as we had no life jackets or helmets. We camped out every night and viewed a lot of the Valley between the Blue Ridge Mountains and the Massanutten range where the South Fork runs.

Section XII: Epilogue

VENTURING OUT OF THE VALLEY

In the next three summers I left the Valley for three wonderful and broadening adventures. I did not know at the time that these trips set the stage for the gradual realization during my life, after many subsequent trips to various places in the States and around the world, that I would discover no place better than the Valley of Virginia.

The first of these trips in 1955 was another young man's adventure. Another close Staunton and VMI friend, Charlie Kellogg, and I bought a 1940 Ford "Woody" station wagon, painted it red, white and yellow for VMI and printed on a red tire cover on the rear, "California or Bust!" I couldn't begin here to relate all of our adventures traversing the country. We mooched off of family friends and families of girl friends, mostly from Mary Baldwin College, all across the country. About half the time we slept in the car. It took six weeks and one of the highlights was staying with Senator Barry Goldwater's family, whom Charlie's mother had known while living in Phoenix, at their house in La Jolla.

I spent the summer of 1956 at ROTC camp at Fort Meade, Maryland, and Fort A. P. Hill, Virginia, where I got my first exposure to the real Army. My last youthful trip in 1957 was a broadening one "on the continent," as they say. An English professor at VMI, the late Colonel Herbert N. Dillard, better known to the cadets as "Dodo," organized it. We sailed from New York on the "Independence" and returned on the "Constitution." Our group was composed of six cadets, five of whom were my classmates, and Colonel Dillard. The trip lasted six weeks and we visited all the major countries in Europe traveling mostly in a Volkswagen van with a driver-guide. I financed the trip with a small inheritance from my grandmother, which my Father recommended that I invest. Suffice it to say, its expenditure was the best investment I ever made.

THE LONG ABSENCE

I then went through an extended period of my life away from the Valley. I had moved to Richmond in the fall of 1957 to seek my fortune and it was there I met my wife to be, Sis. We married in 1960 and produced four children while I was

Section XII: Epilogue

trying to climb the banking ladder. Richmond, which at that time retained its Southern culture and sociability but was a big town for a country boy, became a wonderful home.

in 1973, after I became president of a company named Transohio Financial Corporation, we lived in Ohio for seven years, where we began our experiences of living on farms. I think I inherited some farming genes, as my grandfather owned a farm outside of Staunton where my dad was raised. I also have my dad's love of business and finance, but his love of the military did not take with me. My late brother, to the contrary, went to West Point and spent his career in the Air Force. My Mother's father must also have contributed to my business interest as he was the president of Staunton's National Valley Bank and owned Worthington Hardware. Although it has not been a hardware store for many decades, the sign still hangs at the location on West Beverly Street.

Sis and I laugh about finding our first farm outside of Granville, Ohio, a small delightful town where Denison University is located. It was situated on beautiful rolling land, and she claims I said, "It looks like the Shenandoah Valley without the mountains." In 1976 I moved the headquarters of Transohio to Cleveland and bought a small farm in Hudson, a town southeast of Cleveland that looked like it had been transplanted from New England.

My periodic excursions to the Valley during my Ohio stint were mostly to Camp Mont Shenandoah, a summer girls' camp on the Cowpasture River in Bath County that dates back to the 1920's. My mother-in-law, Mary Lib Cabell (Patrick) Groff, from Charleston, West Virginia, was part of a group who bought it in 1948. In 1967, I put together a small group, including Sis, to acquire the camp from them. In 1972, I acquired an additional 13.5 acres contiguous to the camp on the Cowpasture and long held a dream of building a cabin on it. Sis and my daughter, Ann, bought out the other shareholders in the mid-1990's and Ann has served since as the full time director. The final pay off: Ann has built a handsome house and stable on my adjacent acreage thereby fulfilling my dream 37 years later in a better fashion than I could have imagined.

Section XII: Epilogue

RETURN OF THE VALLEY BOY

In the musical Les Misérable, the main character, Jean Valjean, sings a lilting tenor solo as he is dying, "Take me home." I wasn't dying yet but the circle was complete and I came home when I returned to Lexington in 1978. I was back on the ground where I belonged and where I indeed expect to die. (As Woody Allen said, "None of us are going to get out of this thing alive.") As indicated in the Introduction, we lived on the VMI Post for ten years. For the better part of that time I, not only to satisfy my farming instincts but more importantly to sink tangible roots back into the Valley, purchased the farm near Goshen. It not only was a wonderful family escape place, it provided my farming fix as I raised cattle, had some horses and grew corn. Fortunately, I had a farm manager who knew what he was doing.

The ultimate act of investing in and staking out my instinctive love of the Valley came with the previously described purchase of Peniel Farm and building our dream house where my fixation on House Mountain matured and came to fruition.

THE FINAL WORD

My perception of House Mountain, which I view not only in its uniqueness as the iconic symbol of Lexington, but as a metaphor for my sense of the forces of everlasting beauty and majesty of the Great Valley, may be unique. However, I don't think that to appreciate it fully one need to have had all the experiences in the Valley that I have had, much less carried on an affair with House Mountain. There are countless people who have visited or moved here for the appealing characteristics I have tried to articulate. I speak for them also when I say that we are of the Valley, if not always in residence, always in mind.

Section XII: Epilogue

Shakespeare sums it all up for me personally when he says in King Lear:

> *Men must endure their going hence*
> *even as their coming hither.*
> *Ripeness is all.*

As I complete this book in mid 2015, I look back on much going hence and coming hither in my almost eighty years, and realize that my claim to ripeness in life, both tangible and spiritual, has predominately evolved and been fulfilled in the Valley of Virginia, and its companion mountains.

Further, I have taken pleasure from my fanciful proxy of that truth - a House Mountain Affair.

An Illustration Depicting a Celebration of the Great Valley of Virginia.

"A Visit to the Virginian Canaan", *Virginia Illustrated*, 1857, Washington and Lee University Archives

Section XIII
References

Bodie, Charles A., *A History of Rockbridge County*, Rockbridge Historical Society, 2011.

Boley, Henry, *Lexington in Old Virginia*, Garrett & Massie, Incorporated, 1935.

Couper, Colonel William, *History of the Shenandoah Valley*, Lewis Historical Publishing Company, New York, 1952.

Crayon, Porter, *A Visit to the Virginia Canaan*, Virginia Illustrated, Harper & Brothers, Publishers, New York, 1857.

Dean, Sam, *Geological puzzle poses challenge for hikers*, (Devils Marbleyard), The Roanoke Times, March 13, 2012.

Fox, Emmett, Around the Year with Emmet Fox, Harper & Row, New York, 1935.

Funk, William H., *Return of a Native: The Virginia Elk*, Virginia Wildlife, November/December 2013.

Gupton, Oscar W. and Swope, Fred C., of the VMI Biology Department, *Trees and Shrubs of Virginia*, University Press of Virginia, Charlottesville, 1981.

Guzy, Dan, The 1736 *Survey of the Potomac River*, Virginia Magazine of History and Biography, Vol. 122 No. 1, published by the Virginia Historical Society.

Henry, Thornton M. and Keys, Ruth Henry, *Rockbridge Heritage*, Harmony House Publishers, Louisville, 2004.

Hoyt, William D., *Valley Views 1924 - 1940*, prints by Martin J. Horgan, 1989.

Section XIII: References

Jefferson, Thomas, *Notes on the State of Virginia*, John Stockdale, London, 1787.

Lyle, Royster, *A Wild Garden*, circa 1999, Rockbridge.net.

McClung, Anne Drake, *Among These Ancient Mountains, The Story of Rockbridge County, Virginia*, Alone Mill Publishing, 2001.

McClung, James W., *Historical Significance of Rockbridge County, Virginia*, McClure Co. Inc., Staunton, VA, 1939.

Morton, Oren F., *A History of Rockbridge County*, The McClure Co., Inc., Staunton, Virginia, 1920.

Moyer, Laura, *For Sale: proximity to heaven on earth*, Roanoke Times & World News, November 27, 1988.

The New English Bible, Oxford Study Edition, Oxford University Press, 1976.

Quran, mid-7th Century.

Rouse, Parke W., Jr., *The Great Wagon Road*, Dietz Press, Richmond, 1995.

Spencer, Edgar, *Guidebook to the Natural Bridge and the Natural Bridge Caverns*, Poorhouse Mountain Studios, 1985.

Stevens, Sharon Ritenour and Williams, Alice Trump, *Images of America, Lexington*, Rockbridge Historical Society, Arcadia Publishing, 2009.

Strong, James, Strong's *Exhaustive Concordance of the Bible*, Hendrickson Publishers, Peabody, Massachusetts, 1890.

Wilkes, G. P., Spencer, E. W., Evans, N. H., McCampbell, E. V, *Geology of Rockbridge County, Virginia* Department of Mines, Minerals and Energy, Publication 170, 2007.

Section XIII: References

"Great things are done when men and mountains meet."

William Blake

Mountains seem to answer an increasing imaginative need in the West. More and more people are discovering a desire for them, and a powerful solace in them. At bottom, mountains, like all wildernesses, challenge our complacent conviction - so easy to lapse into - that the world has been made for humans by humans. Most of us exist for most of the time in worlds which are humanly arranged, themed and controlled. One forgets that there are environments which do not respond to the flick of a switch or the twist of a dial, and which have their own rhythms and orders of existence. Mountains correct this amnesia. By speaking of greater forces than we can possibly invoke, and by confronting us with greater spans of time than we can possibly envisage, mountains refute our excessive trust in the man-made. They pose profound questions about our durability and the importance of our schemes. They induce, I suppose, a modesty in us.

Robert Macfarlane, *Mountains of the Mind: Adventures in Reaching the Summit*